Odd

OF A LIFETIME

(Or rather… some poems wot I 'ave writ)

Best Wishes.
Ann Chance

Written by Ann Chance
Illustrated by Julie Willis

First Published in Great Britain in 2008 by Tucann Books
Text © Ann Chance
Illustrations © Julie Willis
All rights reserved
Design © TUCANN*design&print*

ISBN 978-1-873257-87-6

Produced by: TUCANN*design&print*
19 High Street, Heighington, Lincoln LN4 1RG
Tel & Fax: 01522 790009
www.tucann.co.uk

CONTENTS

I'M TRYING TO PASS MY P.P.L. (PRIVATE PILOT'S LICENSE)

You see the weather's gorgeous 'cos today is not my test.
I think the Gods don't love me, and I'm truly not impressed.
I don't ask much, just sun and sky,
With wispy clouds away on high.
A gentle breeze to cool me down,
So I can fly right into town.

Now come on all you weather men,
Stop sending winds of gale force 10,
With nimbus clouds so black and thick,
And turbulence that makes me sick.

An hour and a half of weather fine,
Is all I need to pass this time,
My N.F.T. 3 times I've missed,
I'm now going out to get Brahms and Liszt.

NEVER DRIVE YOUR SONS'CAR

You'll be glad to know that I'm alright,
Although I've had an awful fright.
I know my son was very glum
When he found out what I had done.
I've learnt next time I need a coach, don't go to all that fuss,
Just wave an arm, pay the fare and board it like the rest of us.

BUST REDUCTION

I hear you've had a bust reduction,
Which could be followed by Lipo suction?
A sneaky way of getting thinner,
Mere mortals have to eat less dinner.
Although you're sore a LITTLE bit,
It' nice to know your bra will fit.
Enjoy the clothes you feel you must,
Go out and buy to house the bust,
That's now so small and trim and neat,
Perhaps you could ask if they'd do my feet.
So when you're well we'll share a tipple,
To celebrate your new found nipple.

MARRIED AT LAST
BUT STILL LEARNING.
Can be sung to the tune of "Sweet Betsy from Pyke"

Now all you good people, who are here today,
Have witnessed a Wedding and seen much fair play,
They're off on their own, just starting the quest,
To bride and to groom, we wish you all the best.

Advice on your first night we must offer you.
For if you are nervous and forget what to do.
Just phone up your Dad and he'll give you advice,
And try to convince you it's really quite nice.

The first year of marriage is often a strain,
But love will not fade if you kindle the flame,
Wise men agree that the key to success,
When the man says, "What about it?" The woman says "Yes"

At cooking, the bride, she is not very good,
Her eggs are improving; her coffee's like MUD,
She knows not the difference Twix fat, oil or Trex,
And there's far more to marriage than sex, sex and sex.

The song has now finished and we've had some fun,
Your marriage has started, your world just begun.
We wish to the groom and also his wife,
Love, health and happiness all of their life.

MY FIRST BORING BOARD OF MANAGEMENT MEETING

I've attended my first Board of Management meeting.
Tho' I say it myself, I received quite a greeting.
The very first "Lady", or so I am told,
You "fellers" are loverly, with hearts made of gold.
I'll never forget my first trip to "Brum".
'Cos for six solid hours I sat down IN THE BOARD ROOM.

The Board of Management meeting started promptly on the dot,
The men took off their jackets 'cos the room was very hot.
We drank a cup of coffee just to keep us all awake,
And to help us with decisions that we always have to make.

You should have seen the pile of papers lying on the table.
I'm trying very hard to read them all, but I'm not able.
It looks as if today that we shall all work very hard.
It's a good job that I am the only British Hardware Bard.

We next broke off for lunch and had a lovely lot of fodder,
The Chairman banged his gavel hard and called us back to "odder".
With thirty three more items left to talk about today.
It could be ten o'clock tonight before we get away.

AT LAST, we've reached the item labelled Any Other Business.
I think we've nearly finished and I'm weary you can guess.
You name it and we've talked about it almost all the day.
We do it all for love you know, and don't get any pay.

MY LAST 'BORED' MEETING

Farewell to you all with a lump in my throat,
Some of you'll miss me and some of you'll gloat.
I came here a twit and I almost still am,
When I wanted to speak, my mouth shut like a clam.
I shall leave here today tho' I don't want to go.
So all I can say is "Goodbye Cheerio".

ODE TO WELSH BATH MANUFACTURER

Dear Mr. Glynwed please help me you must,
In you I have put all my faith and my trust,
For three smelly months now I've not had a bath,
If you think that's funny I dare you to laugh.
The toilet is in and the wash basin too,
I've tried, but I can't fit my feet in the loo.
The tiles on the wall look so lonely and sad,
If the bath was there too it wouldn't look bad,
My friends they ignore me, I cannot think why,
I know you could get me a bath if you try,
An effort is needed so please mend your ways,
Remember the universe took just seven days.
With eager excitement I await your reply,
O' give me a bath in which I can lie.

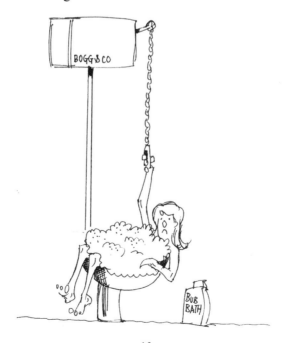

THE REPLY FROM VOGUE BATHROOMS

Your letter was amusing, but the situation's not,
When we keep people waiting they're inclined to get quite hot,
Underneath the collar which we all do understand,
But the volume of our orders is getting out of hand.
But since your rhyming letter has truly struck my heart,
I felt obliged at last and tried my best to do my part.
Just to make it more effective I went down upon one knee.
The casting it was ready and enamelled with great care,
The bath was then inspected, reject it if you dare.
The inspector he was sorry, "The enamel, it's not right
It's looking very patchy, no good in broad daylight".

Rejection stamp upon the bath he at once put into place,
Now I'm left standing here with egg upon my face.
A search of the foundry was started anew,
For a 'Caribbean in Autumn' of the right size and hue.
Our stocks are much depleted and the cupboards are quite bare,
We found one at last to quell my despair.
It's now on a lorry all set for dispatch
And my fingers are crossed that it won't get a scratch.
We're sorry your tiles are so lonely and sad,
But how could they welcome a bath that looked bad.
We're sorry your friends now think you're a fright,
It would have been simpler if your bath had been white.
I know when it's finished you'll be over the moon.
And invite all your friends round your bathroom to view.
With lovely new bath, wash basin and loo.

THE SURGEON GOT CARRIED AWAY

I've heard it on the grapevine and I'm sure it must be true,
That you've misplaced your coxyx and you don't know what to do.
If that is all you've lost, then I think you're very lucky,
But check all your equipment, or I'll have to call you "ducky".

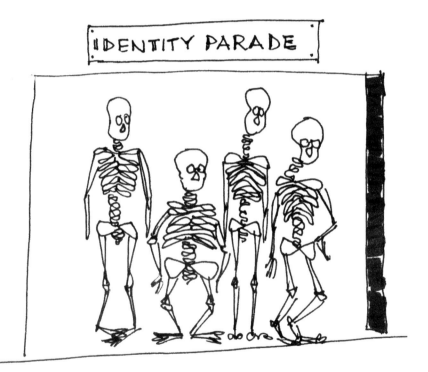

50 YEARS OF MARRIAGE
What the hell do I buy?

It might not take much, but it took quite a time,
To first choose a present and then write this rhyme.
I studied your picture of a cute him and her,
And at once I could see you both as you were.

To think what to buy, set my heart in a whirl.
I thought of a diamond but never a pearl.
Of this rolling pins' use no doubt you're aware,
As for 50 long years it has parted his hair.

WOW!!
50 YEARS AS HUSBAND AND WIFE

The 50 short years you've shared with each other,
A wife, a Mum and also a lover,
A Husband, a Dad, a true friend indeed,
Your lives spent in giving the love you both need.
If all in the world were as happy as you,
Then love and romance would always be new.

WE SHOPKEEPERS
WORK VERY HARD

Phew! It's been a hectic day,
Like a mad house one might say,
Customers waiting at the door,
Just had time to sweep the floor,
Rushing here and rushing there,
People spending without a care.
We've been as they say as busy as bees,
I've worn my legs down to my knees.
But although I'm glad the days is done,
I must admit it's been quite fun.
So think of this day in years when I'm gone.
And remember me kindly as quietly look on,
At the words on my tombstone neatly lacquered
Here lies Eileen Bl…y knackered.

HOW TO LOSE YOUR FRIEND, IN 3 EASY LESSONS

I left my car in Chalfont with a friend to take a ride,
'Cos to drive myself to Brum would make me nervous, I'll confide.
The weather was appalling, there was fog and there was rain,
So to cheer us up we played some tapes and sang a sweet refrain.
Then suddenly it all went wrong, there was tape all round the car,
I picked it up, a mile at least, it really was bizarre.

The meeting done, we said farewell and dashed out in the rain,
A friend of mine sat in the car, he really did complain.
The seat was wet and so was he; he said "It isn't funny".
I'd left the window open and the weather wasn't sunny.
I apologised profusely as I tried to dry him out.
He tried to put my mind at ease; he was cross there was no doubt.

The water mopped, the car dried out, I sat on a polythene bag.
It was not my day, for then I saw in my tights there was a snag.
The journey done, with sigh of relief we're home and in one piece.
And then I saw what made my friends' blood pressure start to increase.
The dye in the bag had all come out and covered his new leather seat.
I said, "Thanks for the lift, we'll do it again", and then beat a hasty
retreat.

THIS ACTUALLY HAPPENED ONE WINDY DAY

In Eastbourne as I strolled one day,
A greyhound happened to blow my way.
He must have thought, here comes the hare,
And rushed right in without a care.
So now next time I take a stroll,
I'll keep both knees under strict control.
It's 10 to 1 the dog's been backed.
I'm back at home with my bits in tact.

YOUR CAR DID WHAT?

The man who works for Kalamazoo
Bought a car, he thought to be new.
He went for a drive and thought it quite queer,
He tried to turn, but it would not steer.
Up on the ramp, the mechanic he said.
"It's lucky for you; I'm surprised you're not dead.
The body and chassis I'm afraid are not one".
So look here you workers, just see what you've done,
And remember the driver named Jonathan White,
Whose chassis went left and whose body went right.

60 YEARS YOUNG

I hear you've reached the magic age,
You know it's time to turn the page.
We Senior Citizens must all join together,
And live out our lives going hell bent for leather.
So welcome to this high class club,
It's happened now..........'aye there's the rub.

OOOPS IT WAS 40 YEARS NOT 25

Dear Mr. and Mrs don't be cross at presents wot I bought.
I wrapped them up quite blasé, and never gave a thought.
Its silver things for 25 and you've been married 40,
I've made a boob I do regret, I'm really very naughty.
In 1965 the silver presents that you had,
Must almost be forgotten, this must make them very sad.
I bought these silver presents with this very thought in mind.
I looked for days for something red, I really couldn't find.
But then I thought they're rather nice, I hope you will agree,
And accept these gifts with lots of love to you and yours from me.

THE TALE OF THE MAGIC ROUNDABOUT (A COUNCIL BLUNDER)

Four poems written to celebrate the unwisely placed mini-roundabout in
the middle of Kingston Road dual carriageway
You could sing along to the tune of "Phil the Fluters' ball
accompanied by Epsom and Ewell Silver Band.

Have you heard the tragic story of the Magic roundabout?
Whenever you go round it you'll be lucky to get out.
Of all the mangled cars there are a lying in a heap.
It's enough to make insurance men sit down and have a weep.

The articulated lorries they go round and round the roundabout,
In and out the gears they go you hear without a doubt,
The lights installed are pretty but they're not yet lit,
This could be why the roundabout is hit.

With a crash in the night that disturbs my beauty sleep OH!
Dashing down with broom in hand the mess I have to sweep,
Oh! BOLLARDS, signposts are scattered far and wide.
I am sure that all the motorists are really not cross-eyed.

There's a 3 2 1 and Give Way sign along the great highway.
They're all knocked down religiously every other day,
So to make it seem quite safe for all, some garden they may take,
For to get around this roundabout you need to be a snake.

So how to put this matter right we really do not know,
Perhaps you could remove it and restore the Status Quo.
The money that would then be saved would help to ease the strife,
Then we'd all be better off I'm sure to lead a happy life.

Now to all the men who helped to build the island in the road,
A Merry Christmas to you all, observe the Highway Code,
Your new year's resolution could include some thoughts perhaps
Like to take away this roundabout and open up the gaps.

STILL GOING ROUND AND ROUND

I hear this Magic Roundabout will soon be elliptical,
The only thing I know that shape is a well used rugby ball.
Perhaps like Eddie Waring, we can now go up and under.
Then all the general public will not notice Councils' blunder.

I see the signs are now in place, they're almost 10 feet tall,
Let's hope these new improvements will protect my garden wall.
It's plain to see you're trying hard, but who will foot the bill?
I bet it's paid by local folk; we're out of pocket still.

Won't someone lend an ear, you know we do not ask for much.
Perhaps the local Council join with Surrey and go Dutch.
Install crash barriers where we ask, it's really very plain,
'Cos to live here now without them, we must almost be insane.

So for three long years I've tried to show the error of your ways,
The fact that you'll not listen, leaves my mind in such a daze.
So as I've said, MY WALL STAYS DOWN, until you all agree,
That the barriers will be fitted with a written guarantee.

29

TAKE IT AWAY, SAID ZEBEDEE!

This badly sited roundabout,
Is a pain in the neck without a doubt?
Before it came we were quite content,
If only we'd known just what it meant.

Over a mile extra we travel each time,
We're all made to suffer: we think it's a crime.
The number of accidents, at least three a week,
Make the prospect of living remarkably bleak.

Who gives you the right to ruin our life?
In this world already there's quite enough strife.
The tradesmen and shoppers are exceedingly cross,
You know that a rolling stone gathers no moss.

The money that's spent every week on repairs,
Makes all of us wonder if anyone cares,
If those who designed it lived here on the spot,
They'd soon all agree, GOOD DESIGN it was not.

So swallow your pride, admit you were wrong,
And please put it right, but don't wait too long.
But if you defer in making this choice,
We'll take you to court, and then you'll hear our voice.

IT'S GONE. BOING!

The Magic Roundabout has gone to bed you must agree,
We haven't had an accident for weeks that you can see.
But has our road been quiet? Oh no, not bloody likely,
You think that Concorde's noisy! We live a life of Reilly.

When traffic moves at quite a pace it lifts the tarmac off,
It sounds as though it's raining, but all we do is cough.
It covers cars and people and all our stock alike,
There's more dust on our bit of road than in the old Klondike.

Now when traffic doesn't move, the problem's not the same,
The sun shines down, the tar gets hot, and it really is a shame,
So when perhaps our road is well and all your mess has gone,
We'll line the route, put out the flags and admire the Phenomenon.

If you could send a team of men to wash the dirt away,
We might perhaps forgive you all the mess and disarray.
But, if you persist to use our road and treat it as a slum.
You will smell the blood of an Englishman, Fee, Fi, Fo, Fum.

Your reply to me came as a shock, you're doing it again.
I don't think I can stand it, it's proving quite a strain.
So come on all you Council men, please get it right this time,
Cos if you don't, I'll make you suffer and compose another rhyme.

ODE TO NARCISSISM
Well, did you know what it meant?

I've watched the numerous Garden Shows that fill our T.V. screens.
I've learnt to nurture all my plants and what to do with beans.
I even know just what to do with bugs and weeds and pests,
And always when it's windy, I put on my woolly vest.

I must confess I'm baffled by the word I have to rhyme.
If I could find out what it meant, I'd use it all the time.
The plural of narcissus has to be narcissisms
But as I don't know what it means I don't know if I'd missisism.

But wait a mo' I've found the word is not what I had thought,
I'm really quite embarrassed and a little bit distraught.
I now know that it means to love your body and yourself,
So I'll practise narcissism not to be left on the shelf.

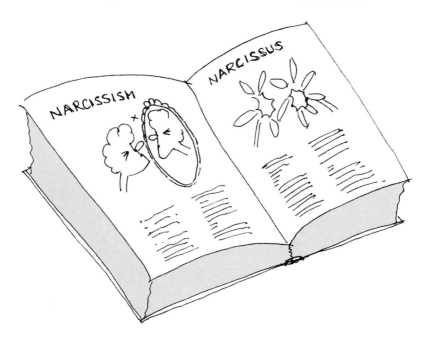

COME TO MY CONFERENCE IN PARADISE

I extend a welcome to one and all,
To come with me to Portugal.
Enjoy the food, the wines, and the sun.
The beaches, the people, they're second to none.
The business I promise will be worthwhile,
The fun we will have will make you all smile.
I couldn't have chosen a better spot.
So take "A CHANCE" it's got the lot.

Each room 1st class with grand sea view.
Two beds, two basins, a bidet and loo.
A bath, a shower, a table, a light,
A balcony too, what a wonderful sight.
I'm much impressed with all I've seen
I have to confess I'm much more than keen.
I couldn't have chosen a better spot,
So take "A CHANCE" it's got the lot.

Two pools, a sauna, a keep fit gym,
A hairdressing salon for her and for him.
A bus that is free goes into the town,
Perhaps to the beach, where you can get brown.
There's many a bar and places to meet,
And lots of exciting things you can eat.
I couldn't have chosen a better spot,
So take "A CHANCE" it's got the lot.

ODE TO VASECTOMY

I hear you're having the final chop,
For quite a few days your pleasure must stop.
But when you are better,
You'll be a trend setter,
Enjoying the freedom with careful bliss,
Without all the parts that you'll never miss.

WOW!! 21 TODAY

Today's the day you're twenty one.
For you, your life has just begun.
When you were one,
You were a bundle of fun.

When you were three,
You sat on my knee.
When you were four,
Your clothes you tore.

When you were eight,
You stayed up late.
When you were nine,
You were looking fine.
When you were ten
You wondered when,
You'd ever be,
A great big "HE".

And then at last you're in your teens,
You dress all day in tatty jeans.
Just then one day you wake to find,
There's another sex, the opposite kind.
You stay out late and have a ball,
And kiss and snog in your mothers' hall.
So now that you are twenty one,
You're in no doubt, life has just begun.

THAT DAMNED
TICKET PRICING MACHINE

Your ticket machine is a lovely tool,
9 times out of 10 it works to rule,
Just when you think it's going great,
It goes on strike with malicious hate,
I talk to it nicely in loving tones,
It repays me quite badly; it just grunts and groans.
The tickets fly out at every angle,
Some of them dingle, but most of them dangle.
If I had a machine that worked all the time,
Then I wouldn't have had to write you this rhyme.

OUCH! I BET THAT MADE YOU WINCE

Your Polypus has had the chop.
For just a few days your pleasure must stop.
But when you are well and really feel great,
You'll return to your husband, your lover, your mate,
Refreshed in the thought that you're free from all strife,
Returned to your husband as a new sexy wife.

OH!! BUNIONS

I looked at both my feet they were ugly, fat and crooked,
I telephoned the hospital my visit time to book it.
The surgeon said, "You've Bunions and they really are a pest".
"You need to come in now to take at least a week of rest".
So when at last my feet are well and all the bumps deplete,
I can wear what pair of shoes I like on my new found plates of meat.

41

ODE TO THE TAXMAN

If all the money that I'd earned was underneath the bed,
I wouldn't live in Ewell and at the Bank be in the red.
But alas for me you've noticed where I've hidden all the cash.
I'm sorry no, not know, no time, I've really got to dash,
To foreign climes where Income Tax is not a dirty word,
Or keeping all your hard earned cash is not thought so absurd.
So come on all you taxmen, git your fingers off my dough,
I've told you once; I've told you twice, the answer is still NO!

A DITTY FOR THE DOMESTIC WHO DIDN'T DUST

Please clean the bath, the basin, the loo
And then I'll pay you what you're due.
There are cobwebs here and cobwebs there,
They spin their webs without a care.
Please make my house look spic and span
With the "Help" of my dog, do the best that you can.

50 YEARS OF MARRIED BLISS

It' some 50 years since this couple first met.
They both came from Balham, the upper crust set.
Twas love at first sight, so they soon named the day,
And promised to honour and love and obey.

X

The groom played the piano in days of his youth.
He too played accordion in that there's some truth.
A dance band in Streatham is where he hung out,
Was slow slow, quick quick, slow of that there's no doubt.

The bride when a young girl,
learnt how to perm hair,
She cut it and curled it till clients were bare.
The ministry of shipping will ne'er be the same,
'Cos during the war that's where she rose to fame.

The local fire service is where our groom Stan,
Will tell many stories, if remember he can,
The punch lines are hazy, the last lines forgot,
Are you getting old groom? Oh no, you are not.

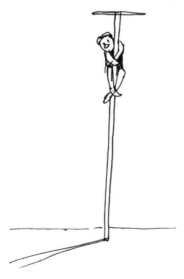

At sewing, the bride she is really quite smart,
Her knitting is awful but it sets her apart.
But give her a raffle to make lots of dough.
In this she'll excel, she is magnifico.

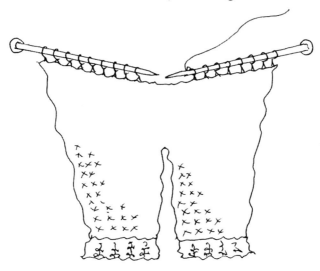

Grooms' hobbies are painting
and croquet I hear,
With mallet in hand he breeds terror and fear,
His painting by numbers
you all must not scoff.
With practice I'm sure they'll
soon look like Van Gogh.

In Inner Wheel our Bride's a force to behold,
In Towns Women's Guild she's the same, but more bold.
For back pain she's also worked hard, long and true,
And served meals on time for her man, wouldn't you?

Throughout their long lives they've had shops old and new,
They've sold fruit and veg and a record or two.
In Kingston-on-Thames ironmongers became,
They didn't wait long before rising to fame.

So just how to finish this story in rhyme,
To the Bride and the Groom you are partners in crime
May all of your days be what you would wish for,
That when this rhyme's finished you'll call for encore.

A RETIREMENT ODE
TO MY LOCAL PRINTER.
O DEER HOO WIL DU MI PRINTIN?

To Mister and Missis your big day has come,
When you can sit legally down on your bum.
No more of those deadlines to get out on time.
You see it's your fault I've written this rhyme.
No posters, no letters, no ink blots on ties,
No broken machinery or you telling lies.
So how will you fill every hour of your day?
Whatever you do, you will do it your way.

"NEWS FLASH"
SUPER HEROES JUMP FROM PLANE FOR CHARITY.

To Batman who was very brave,
For a worthy cause your all you gave.
As Wonder Woman I felt I oughta,
Have been there to turn the fence to water.

In your troubled time when my help you needed,
My crown had slipped and my powers impeded.
The look on your face I will never forget,
As someone went running and brought back a vet.

The Bat mobiles waiting and raring to go.
With the caped crusaders the dynamic trio.
But without you dear Batman, we're lost and alone.
So come on, get better and hurry on home.

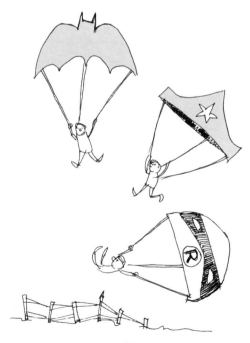

WONDERWOMAN, BATMAN AND ROBIN SAY THANKS TO THEIR PUBLICISTS

To John and Ruth a great big thanks,
For helping with our daring pranks.
The time and effort that you gave,
Has helped rebuild the new Bat Cave.
Without your skill and daring do,
We couldn't have raised such revenue.
So when next time this mood comes o'er me,
I hope you'll do the publicity for me.

GALL STONES ARE
A PAIN IN THE BUTT

Your gall stones are removed I hear,
I bet you let out one big cheer.
Shingle on the beach is right,
But stones inside give you a fright.
They're now in a jar for all to see.
They look just like a Birds Eye Pea.
Your friends are glad that you are well,
The Medics too, so I hear tell.
So let's go out and celebrate,
Good health, long life, from your next door mate.

TO MY FRIENDS - MARRIED 30 YEARS - SO FAR

'Twas thirty years ago, you two became as one,
Just think of all the good things that together you have done.
To share this day with you is such a pleasure for us all,
When we've gone home, I hope your mates still got his wherewithal.
His credentials are in order 'cos your eyes are all aglow,
It's plain to see that you're his girl and he's your dashing beau.

AND THE REPLY CAME BACK...

The memory of our 30th will be ours for ever more,
You all were truly wonderful, good friends down to the core.
We thank you for your lovely gifts; we'll treasure them for years.
Even to the pearl light bulb which will see us through the years.
We'll cut the cake and slice the cheese and serve them on the tray.
Arrange the flowers in the vase to make a good display.
We've captured all upon a film we can recall at will,
We hope that you'll all come again then you can pay the bill.

I HEAR IT COULD BE YOUR BIRTHDAY

A little birdie told me that you've got a birthday soon,
If your Mother hadn't waited, then the next word could be June,
But as things were, she was in charge, July it has to be,
A Happy Birthday neighbour, from all next door and me.

WHERE SHALL WE GO THIS YEAR FOR OUR CONFERENCE?

I first thought of Bermuda, what a lovely placc to be,
Grand Canyon would be smashing with lots of things to see.
I then thought of Jamaica, but I didn't think we'd dare,
I then thought of Hawaii, but we can't afford the fare.
I then thought of Las Vegas, we could gamble every night,
And then sat down to think, you know, I don't think that is right.
So long as we're together, we will have a smashing time,
If I hadn't had this problem, I could not have writ this rhyme.
So whatever place we finally choose, I know it will be great,
And I hope that you'll be with me on this very special date.

HOW NOT TO TREAT A TETRAPLEGIC

On Monday, Wednesday and Friday, I'm allowed to pass a motion,
But what to do on Tuesday, Thursday, Sunday, I've no notion.
Of all the stupid rulings this one really is absurd.
No one dare dictate to me when I can pass a turd.
I've seen the list that shows me all the types that I may pass,
But how to know which one it is when sitting on my arse.
What I perform in private is for my eyes I declare,
And for you to treat me this way is nothing but unfair.
'So why wont all you bosses please observe my private life?
You've over stretched your powers and caused me a lot of strife.

A FIRST IT WAS G.P.O AND THEN B.T.

We'd like to have a phone that works,
And not to suffer annoying quirks.
We pay our bill each month on time,
So please come quick and men our line.

THE GREAT ESCAPE AT 65

This masterpiece wot I 'ave wrote,
Should bring a lump into your 'froat'
You've been my friend 'froo' 'fick' and 'fin'
Remember the time we drank all that gin?
You've got the boot, I'm sorry to say,
But I know I will see you from day to day.
Enjoy yourself, good luck to you,
Have fun and laughter in all you do.

YEEHAH!

AMATEURS, YOU WERE GREAT, WELL, MOST OF YOU

For the work that you did in our show, I am glad,
When all's said and done, we're really not bad.
I hope you enjoyed it, the work is worthwhile.
Our greatest reward is to make people smile.
So I hope if we're asked to do an encore,
I can count on your help to do it once more.

FLYMO USERS, BEWARE

I send to you this tube of glue,
To make your toes as good as new,
And when next time you mow the grass,
Try not to fall upon your arse.

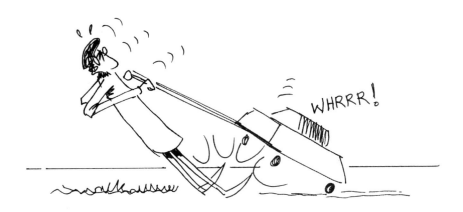

ODE TO CONDOMS

I hear that all your condoms come in sizes large to small,
I wrote a letter, weeks ago, no response I've had at all.
Your customer care is lacking and I don't know what to do.
And if I was not disabled then like you I'd use the loo,
But as it is I'm wheelchair bound and need a helping hand,
In choosing sizes best for me, from small through large to grand.

THIS IS WHAT TO DO AFTER YET ANOTHER HEART ATTACK

You heard of my "turn" I only had it you see,
To first get an ode and perhaps sympathy,
So instead of a letter I'm sending this ode,
'Cos I'm feeling much better and back on the road.
I took your advice and had plenty of sex,
It was more fun than business and I wasn't so vexed
But after a time I'd had rather a lot
Now I'm back in the ward resting here on my bot.

ANOTHER HEART ATTACK?

I hear you've had another turn.
Amongst your friends there is some concern.
You really must not work so hard,
Or else your good looks will be marred.
There's more to life than making dough,
Just what they are, I'm sure you know.
Relax a while, life's quite complex,
There's one thing left that must be sex.

I DON'T UNDERSTAND BROAD SCOTTISH

I must confess your letter had me baffled for a mo'
The expression "Greetin Faced" about a man I do not know.
But then a Sassenach I am and Balham borne and bred,
If you want to talk in rhyming slang then that I'll teach you Ed.
I thought that you were pure in thought, not swear or be obscene,
But then you Scots are all alike, it's worse in Aberdeen.
Your letter was a smashing one I'll cherish all my life,
My grateful thanks and luv to you and trouble and strife, that's wife.

THE IRONMONGERESS!

To have been the first lady has proved quite a strain,
But if ever I'm asked I'd do it again.
It does a girls' ego a hell of a lot,
To be here on this platform, showing you what I've got,
So how to say thank-you to each of you here,
Perhaps in the bar I could buy you a beer.

To the incoming President I wish you good luck,
What I'm trying to say is I'm passing the buck.
The chain I have worn now for twelve months with pride,
With the help of you all sitting here by my side,
My bosom will always remember the strain,
I shall feel like a lion that has cut off his mane.
My year I've enjoyed and I hope you will too,
Have a wonderful time, cheerio, toodle-oo.

STRANGE HABITS

There once was a WHITE horse called BLUE.
Who whilst on the trot took a "POO".
When the rider said, "GO".
The horse said, "Wait a Mo",
"I've stopped for a POO, wouldn't you?"

WHO SAID WOMEN ALWAYS HAVE A HEADACHE?

As I strolled into an ostrich farm with vigour, poise and grace,
I wasn't long before what happened put a smile upon my face.
A male and female ostrich had decided they would mate,
And this I'd like to mention now took place on their first date.
A headache she did usually have - today she's feeling fine.
So when the ostrich comes to call they'll do it every time

"YE OLDE RED TELEPHONE BOXES" K9S OR K6S

Have you, as a caring member of the human race, ever given so much as a casual thought, to the whereabouts of all the now, beloved, always 'out of service', red telephone boxes?
Are they enjoying a well earned recuperation on a quiet sandy beach somewhere in the south of England?
Perhaps being hosed down twice a day, fed with real food, like 10p pieces and 50p pieces, not plastic food like phone cards.
Gone forever are the happy times, when upon entering a red box, if you were strong enough to open the door, it would close heavily behind you trapping your ankles.
Gone will be the times spent squeezing thirty people into a phone box.
Gone forever is yet another Historical Heritage, known to young and old, a meeting place, a familiar friend, somewhere to eat your chips on a rainy day.
What can be done about our new insignificant yellow/green phone kiosks?
I can understand why they are vandal proof. They are so hard to find. At least when they were red, they could be found, even though upon arrival they were clearly 'out of service', or on a bad day, just a box and no phone.
Come on BT liven up our dull streets, put your thinking caps on.
I think the new boxes are a great improvement, but, let's have some proper co-ordination.
Yellow painted boxes with BLUE telephone!!!!

It's just not British is it?